MW01260165

# Macbeth

## William Shakespeare

## TEACHER GUIDE

**NOTE:**

The trade book edition of the novel used to prepare this guide is found in the Novel Units catalog and on the Novel Units website. Using other editions may have varied page references.

Please note: We have assigned Interest Levels based on our knowledge of the themes and ideas of the books included in the Novel Units sets, however, please assess the appropriateness of this novel or trade book for the age level and maturity of your students prior to reading with them. You know your students best!

**ISBN 978-1-56137-436-6**

To order, contact your
local school supply store, or:

Toll-Free Fax: 877.716.7272
Phone: 888.650.4224
3901 Union Blvd., Suite 155
St. Louis, MO 63115

sales@novelunits.com

novelunits.com

# Table of Contents

# Introduction

**To the Teacher:** The background information on William Shakespeare and on the Globe Theatre are given to use as you choose—either as lecture notes or as supplemental material after students have completed the suggested Cooperative Research project on page 5.

## William Shakespeare

One of the great mysteries of English drama is that so little is known for sure about one of its most famous playwrights. Fact became mingled with legend in the 100 years after Shakespeare's death, and it was not until then that any biographical information was recorded.

Shakespeare's exact birth date is unknown, but he was baptized on April 26, 1564, in Stratford-on-Avon, England. His father, John, was a prosperous wool, leather, and grain merchant as well as a town official. His mother, Mary, was the daughter of a gentleman farmer. It is known that young William attended school and studied Latin and literature. In 1582, he married Anne Hathaway, a woman eight years his senior. They had three children: a daughter, Susanna, and twins Hamnet and Judeth.

In 1586, Shakespeare left Stratford to become the stage manager of The Theatre in London, so named because it was the only theatre in town. He soon joined the acting company of The Theatre, and with Richard Burbage and William Kemp he performed at court in many plays.

Shakespeare's earliest works were produced in 1591-92, including several of the histories and *Love's Labour's Lost*, *Two Gentlemen of Verona*, and *Comedy of Errors*. In 1592, he wrote *Romeo and Juliet*. It was followed in quick succession by *The Merchant of Venice*, *A Midsummer Night's Dream*, *All's Well That Ends Well*, *The Taming of the Shrew*, and *The Merry Wives of Windsor*.

Shakespeare made an important business move in 1599 when he joined Richard Burbage and several other actors and built the Globe Theatre. He was a shareholder in the Globe and a part-owner of a company of actors called Lord Chamberlain's Company, later known as The King's Men.

Many of Shakespeare's plays were produced at the Globe, where he had both financial security and a first-rate acting company to produce his plays. This was his greatest writing period. In 1599-1600 he wrote *Much Ado about Nothing*, *As You Like It*, and *Twelfth Night*. Between 1600 and 1611, he wrote the tragedies for which he is so well remembered: *Julius Caesar, Hamlet, Othello, Macbeth, King Lear,* and *Antony and Cleopatra*, among others. During this time he also wrote 154 sonnets which were published in 1609. Late in 1608 or 1609, Shakespeare and his partners purchased the Blackfriars Theatre to use as a winter location for play production.

In 1611, at the height of his fame and popularity, Shakespeare moved back to Stratford. His son died at this time. He sold out his interests in London, although he did continue to write and travel to the city until his death in 1616.

**The Globe Theatre**

To visualize Shakespeare's theatre, imagine a small football stadium with a roof over the seats and a stage extending from one end out into the center of the field. Part of the stage and the area around it would be a raised platform. Curtains were pulled across the rear of the stage, but the open area in front could be seen at all times. It represented a variety of locations, indoors and out.

With little or no scenery, the audience had to rely on previous knowledge or upon the actors' words to locate the action. The play could move rapidly since there were no changes of scenery. Even a long play like Romeo and Juliet could be presented in two hours.

Plays were presented in daylight hours, and no spectator sat more than 60 feet from the stage. As a result of this intimacy with the audience, certain dramatic conventions developed. One was the aside, in which an actor confided his true thoughts and feelings directly to the audience while the other actors on stage pretended not to hear. Another was the soliloquy, in which an actor alone on stage spoke aloud his private thoughts.

**Note:** The edition of *Macbeth* used to prepare this guide was the softcover Pelican Shakespeare, edited by Alfred Harbage and published by the Penguin Group. It was chosen because of its faithfulness to the original Shakespeare, and its excellent footnotes. References to act and scene numbers should coincide with all editions. If you are using a version in a secondary textbook, you may find that the language does not exactly match in some instances.

# Shakespeare's Background and the Globe Theatre

Welcome to the world of Elizabethan drama! For the next week, you will work in groups to learn the material necessary for a complete understanding of William Shakespeare's background and the environment in which his plays were produced.

**Write the names of your group's members below:**

_____          _____

_____          _____

_____          _____

_____          _____

Each group is responsible for learning about Shakespeare's life, his writings, and the Globe Theatre. Each member of the group is responsible for creating a visual aid and a handout (outline, notes, etc.) with a bibliography of materials that you used to obtain your facts and that others may consult for more information. Make five copies of your handout.

Now, next to each group member's name, write the number of the topic for which he or she will be responsible

1. Shakespeare's Life
2. Shakespeare's comedies and histories
3. The Globe Theatre
4. Shakespeare's tragedies and poetry

**Schedule:**

**Days 1 and 2:** Spend both days in the library researching your topics. Stay in your group on Day 1. On Day 2, work with someone from another group who has the same topic as you do.

**Day 3:** Spend in class with a member from another group with the same topic. Work together to revise your handouts and visual aids and to practice your presentation.

**Day 4:** Spend in your group sharing information. Provide handouts and display your visual aid(s).

# Plot Summary

## Act I

Three witches on a barren Scottish heath await Macbeth, the Thane of Glamis. On a battlefield nearby, a wounded soldier tells Duncan, the King of Scotland, of the courageous behavior exhibited on the battlefield by Macbeth and his friend, Banquo. Duncan sentences the traitorous Thane of Cawdor to death, and says he will give his title to Macbeth. In the third scene, the three witches greet Macbeth with two titles which baffle him: Thane of Cawdor and King of Scotland. They also tell Banquo he will be the father of kings. The witches vanish, leaving Macbeth and Banquo intrigued. In Scene Four, Ross and Angus, other thanes (lords), inform Macbeth of King Duncan's decision to make him Thane of Cawdor. This confirmation of one of the predictions made by the witches gives Macbeth considerable pause as he thinks that the only way their other prediction could come true would be if Duncan were to die. He pushes the thought away and tells himself he will leave it to chance. Duncan and Macbeth meet in a field, and Macbeth expresses his loyalty and homage, but he is disappointed when Duncan names his son, Malcolm, as successor to the throne. Duncan tells Macbeth he'll visit him at his home, Inverness Castle, that evening. Meanwhile, Lady Macbeth has received a letter from her husband relating the prophecies of the witches. Lady Macbeth, anxious to hasten her husband's coronation, and afraid he is too kind to do so himself, calls on the evil spirits to help her convince him to kill Duncan. When she presents her plan to Macbeth, he vacillates, but she is eventually able to goad him into an agreement. Lady Macbeth will give Duncan's bodyguards drugged wine while Macbeth kills him. The bodyguards will then be blamed for killing the king.

## Act II

Banquo has been bothered by a dream about the "three weird sisters," but when he mentions to Macbeth that they spoke some truth, Macbeth dismisses it. He then has a vision of a bloody dagger. There is a short soliloquy in which we see his horror at what he is about to do, but he proceeds with the plan, stabbing Duncan to death. When he emerges from Duncan's chamber with the two bloody daggers, it is Lady Macbeth who must return them to the sides of the guards, and smear their faces with Duncan's blood. She is practical and calm, while Macbeth raves about what he has done—he will never rest peacefully again, and an ocean of water cannot wash the blood from his hands. Early the next morning, Macduff and Lennox, two of Duncan's loyal followers, arrive. When Macduff discovers Duncan's dead body, Macbeth feigns a grief-stricken rage and kills the two bodyguards. Malcolm and Donalbain, Duncan's sons, grow suspicious and fearful and flee to England and Ireland, resulting in their becoming prime suspects in the murder. Macduff tells Ross that Macbeth has already gone to Scone (Scotland's capital) to be crowned. Ross says he will follow, but Macduff goes back to his home in Fife.

## Act III

Banquo grows suspicious of how Macbeth rose so quickly to the throne, but remains friendly toward Macbeth. Macbeth , however, believes the witches' predictions, and sees Banquo and his son, Fleance, as threats. He hires two murderers to kill them, but Fleance escapes. At a feast that evening, Banquo's ghost appears (visible only to Macbeth). The horrified Macbeth acts so strangely that Lady Macbeth asks the guests to leave, explaining her husband's behavior as a "fit.". Macbeth says he must see the witches as soon as possible. The witches, meanwhile, meet with their mistress, Hecate, to plan Macbeth's downfall. Lennox receives news that Macduff has gone to England to join forces with Malcolm and to enlist the aid of the English king. Although Lennox continues an apparent allegiance to Macbeth, he reveals to another lord that he wishes Malcolm and Macduff success in ousting Macbeth.

## Act IV

Macbeth finds the witches, who show him a procession of apparitions each with a warning for Macbeth. An armed head tells him to beware of Macduff. A bloody child tells him "none of woman born shall harm Macbeth." Another child, holding a tree branch, tells him he will be safe "until Birnam Wood comes to Dunsinane." Finally, Macbeth watches as eight kings appear, followed by Banquo's ghost. The witches vanish, and Lennox appears with the news about Macduff's flight to England. Macbeth immediately plans to attack Macduff's unprotected castle at Fife, killing his wife and children. While Macbeth's orders are being carried out, Malcolm and Macduff meet in England. To test Macduff's loyalty, Malcolm claims that when he is king he will make Macbeth look like a gentle lamb. Macduff's distressed reaction satisfies him. Ross brings word of the murders at Fife, and a distraught Macduff vows to kill Macbeth with his own sword.

## Act V

At Dunsinane—now the residence of the Macbeths—Lady Macbeth has begun sleepwalking. A doctor and one of her ladies in waiting watch as she unconsciously reveals her part in the murder of Duncan and her guilt over the deaths at Fife. Malcolm and Macduff advance on Dunsinane with 10,000 English soldiers. Macbeth feels safe because of the witches' prophecies. He receives the word of Lady Macbeth's demise with little surprise or feeling. Malcolm tells each soldier to carry a bough from the trees in Birnam Wood for camouflage. When Macbeth sees the advancing forest, he feels betrayed by the witches, but the final prediction that no man born of woman shall harm him gives him strength. He kills Young Siward and then battles Macduff, telling him with confidence of his charmed life. Macduff then reveals that his own birth was Caesarean. Although Macbeth fights on, Macduff wins, and carries Macbeth's head victoriously to Malcolm, hailing him as King of Scotland.

# Pre-Reading Activities

1. **T-diagram**
   Have the students react to hypothetical situations analogous to those in the play. For example, "Suppose there is a position you very much want: quarterback, leading role in a play. editor of the yearbook. The only way you can get it is to somehow discredit the person who currently has the position." Have students use a T-diagram to weigh the pros and cons of obtaining the position this way.

2. **Cooperative Activity**
   Divide the students into small groups, and assign each group a word for brainstorming from the list below. They should think of synonyms and antonyms, give examples from the past and present, and add anything else their brainstorming sessions produce. After about ten minutes, have a spokesperson from each group share results with the whole class, and ask for further input.

   • Ambition      • Power      • Guilt      • Ruthlessness

3. **Historical/Shakespearean Comparison**
   Have the students take notes on the information given below concerning the actual Macbeth, King of Scots. On another sheet of paper, have them set up a comparison diagram. As they read the play, they can compare the historical information with Shakespeare's version. Be sure to point out that information about the actual Macbeth is sketchy because he lived so long ago, and actual fact has become mingled with legend.

4. **Geography**
   The map of Scotland which appears on page 10 of this guide can be enlarged on a copier and mounted on poster board. Use it throughout the reading to identify locations of various scenes. It may also be helpful to define the location of Scotland itself on a world map, and to discuss the terrain (primarily mountainous), proximity to the sea (no point in Scotland is further than 70 miles from it), and climate (cold winters, damp, cool summers). As a corollary activity, have the students list things that they connect with Scotland, i.e., bagpipes, kilts, plaids, Scotch whiskey, shortbread, barley and oats, the expression "scotch" meaning "stingy." You might even throw out some extra-credit challenges for students to find out why Scotch tape, Scotch broth, Scottish Terriers, and Scotch mist were thus named.

# Historical Source for *Macbeth*

Shakespeare's primary source for *Macbeth* was Holinshed's *Chronicles of England, Scotland, and Ireland*. Rather than following history as related by Holinshed, Shakespeare combined two separate incidents: Donwald's murder of King Duff in 967 A.D. and Macbeth's murder of Duncan in 1040 A.D. The themes of the power of guilt and evil came from Shakespeare's imagination, since there was no way to know from historical facts how the real Macbeth felt after he wrested the throne from Duncan.

In the first historical incident, King Duff executed several nobleman whom he felt were conspiring against him with the aid of witches. Donwald, a nobleman who objected to the executions, plotted with his wife to kill Duff by making sure his bodyguards drank too much and left Duff unprotected. Donwald paid four servants to cut Duff's throat.

In the second incident recorded by Holinshed, Macbeth and his friend Banquo, on their return from a battle with the Norwegian king, encountered three wild-looking women who predicted that Macbeth would be Thane of Cawdor and King of Scotland, and that Banquo's descendants would be kings. Apparently the real Macbeth took the predictions quite seriously from the start, and began plotting to attain the throne then occupied by the extremely kind and benevolent King Duncan I. Macbeth, with the help of Banquo, soon killed Duncan in battle and proclaimed himself king, causing Duncan's two sons to flee in fear for their own lives.

Macbeth ruled for ten years and was considered a good king, but he was haunted by the prophecy that Banquo's sons would inherit the kingdom. Finally he hired murderers to kill Banquo and his son, Fleance. Banquo died but Fleance escaped. After this incident, Macbeth became ruthless and unpredictable. He feared Macduff so much that he himself killed Macduff's family and banished Macduff from Scotland, calling him a traitor.

Macduff gathered an army and had them advance on Macbeth's castle by using boughs from trees as camouflage. Macduff then beheaded Macbeth and carried his head to Malcolm.

*(As students make comparisons, they should note that it was Donwald's wife who plotted to kill Duff, not Macbeth's; that Banquo was involved in the real death of Duncan while in Shakespeare's version Banquo is "pure"; that Macbeth reigned without tyranny for ten years. Shakespeare also added the cauldron scene with the three witches and Hecate, probably to make the play more exciting to his audiences, most of whom would have firmly believed in the existence of witches.)*

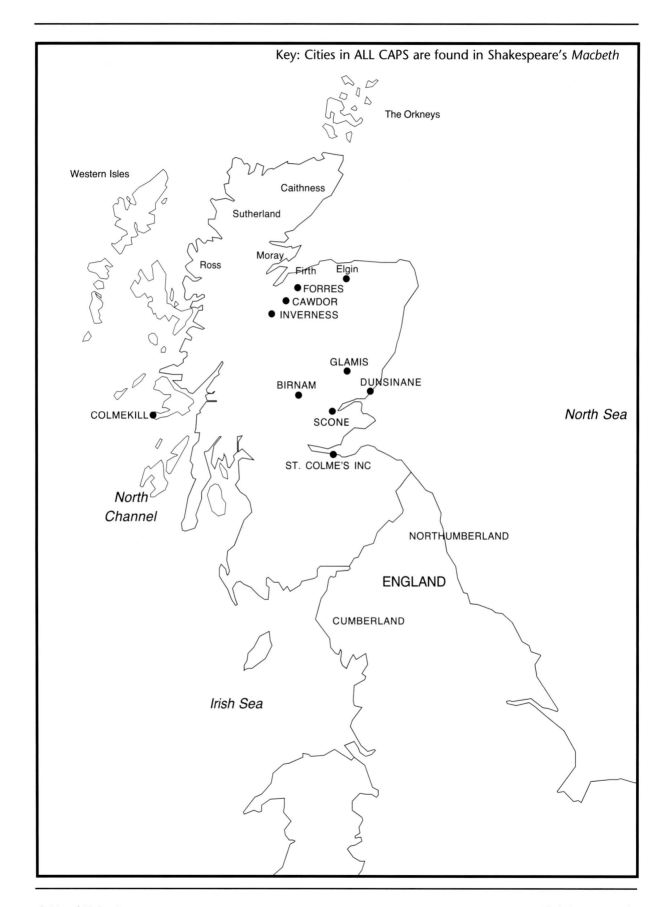

Key: Cities in ALL CAPS are found in Shakespeare's *Macbeth*

The Orkneys

Western Isles

Caithness

Sutherland

Ross

Moray

Firth

Elgin

● FORRES

● CAWDOR

● INVERNESS

GLAMIS
●

BIRNAM
●

DUNSINANE
●

COLMEKILL ●

SCONE
●

North Sea

ST. COLME'S INC
●

North
Channel

NORTHUMBERLAND

ENGLAND

CUMBERLAND

Irish Sea

It will be helpful to students' understanding of the play if they can easily glance at a character chart during the reading. Before reading a scene where a new character is introduced, have students find on the charts his or her name, description, and relationship to other characters. A suggested format follows.

## Main Characters in *Macbeth*

| Character Name/Description: | Introduced in: | |
|---|---|---|
| | Act | Scene |
| The Three Witches (also called "Weird Sisters") | I | i |
| Duncan, King of Scotland, Macbeth's cousin | I | ii |
| Malcolm, elder son of Duncan | I | ii |
| Ross, Scottish nobleman (Thane of Ross) | I | ii |
| Macbeth, Thane (lord) of Glamis, Captain in King's Army | I | iii |
| Banquo, Scottish nobleman, Captain, friend of Macbeth | I | iii |
| Lady Macbeth, Macbeth's wife | I | v |
| Fleance, son of Banquo | II | i |
| Macduff, Scottish nobleman | II | iii |
| Donalbain, younger son of Duncan | II | iii |
| Lennox, Scottish nobleman | II | iii |
| Murderers | III | i |
| Hecate, Queen of the Witches | IV | i |
| Lady Macduff | IV | ii |
| Old Siward, Macduff's father | V | iv |
| Young Siward, Macduff's brother | V | viii |

### Relationships:

**Duncan, King of Scotland**
- Malcolm (son)
- Donalbain (son)

**Macbeth, Thane of Glamis**
- Lady Macbeth (wife)

**Banquo, a Nobleman**
- Fleance (son)

**Old Siward, a Nobleman**
- Young Siward (son)
- Macduff (son)
  - Lady Macduff (wife) ⟶ Ross (her cousin)

# Plot Structure of the Shakespearean Tragedy

Discuss the five-act, seven-element structure of the Shakespearean tragedy with students. A chart designed for use with an overhead projector appears on page 25 of this guide. The student reproducible on page 26 can be used for follow-up.

| | |
|---|---|
| **Act I:** | Exposition, Exciting Force, Rising Action |
| **Act II:** | Rising Action |
| **Act III:** | Rising Action, Climax, Falling Action |
| **Act IV:** | Falling Action |
| **Act V:** | Falling Action, Catastrophe |

*Elements defined:*

1. **Exposition:** The general atmosphere, time, place, main characters, and opening conditions of the play.

2. **Exciting Force:** Something happens that starts the action of the play moving, usually in the first act.

3. **Rising Action:** This is a series of actions usually covering more than one act. During the rising action, the hero of the play (the protagonist) is the active force, trying to make things work out as he or she intended.

4. **Climax:** The protagonist reaches the peak of his or her power and a distinct change occurs in him or her as well as in the direction of the action. Things begin to go against the protagonist, who seems to be following a downward path.

5. **Falling Action:** This also covers several scenes and shows all the ways the main events are going against the main character. At this time, the antagonist begins to rise in power. The conflict between the protagonist and the antagonist becomes the essence of the play.

6. **Moment of Final Suspense:** Usually found in the fifth act of the play, the moment of final suspense has a particular function in the organization of the plot. Close to the end of the play, it is more significant to the protagonist than it is to the audience. It is the moment when things begin to look as if they will go the way of the protagonist again. He or she momentarily believes that tragedy will be averted.

7. **Catastrophe:** This is the complete downfall of the protagonist, either through death or some other devastating circumstance. If the protagonist is a villain, then the catastrophe will be seen by the audience as a good thing.

# Vocabulary • Discussion Questions
# Writing Assignments • Activities

## Act I

### Vocabulary
Since line numbers vary from edition to edition, only the scene numbers are indicated for the vocabulary words. You may find that most words are defined in the footnotes of the text you are using.

| Scene i | Scene iii | Scene iv | Scene vi |
|---|---|---|---|
| hurlyburly | ronyon | liege | seat |
| heath | sieve | toward | hermits |
| | posters | | coursed |
| | attire | | compt |
| | fantastical | | still |
| | rapt | | |
| *Scene ii* | corporal | *Scene v* | *Scene vii* |
| broil | earnest | missives | surcease |
| minion | addition | illness | couriers |
| thane | home | round | supped |
| lavish | imperial theme | ministers | adage |
| | surmise | beguile | prithee |
| | favor | sway | convince |
| | | favor | wassail |
| | | | mettle |

### Questions for Discussion

*Scene i*
1. Who do the witches plan to meet when the battle is over? *(Macbeth)*

2. What kind of mood is established in this scene? *(a foreboding one)*

3. "Man proposes, God disposes" is an example of antithesis from a poem by Alexander Pope. Can you find some other examples in this scene? *("When the battle's lost and won;" "Fair is foul, and foul is fair.")* How do these antitheses emphasize the mood? *(They evoke mystery and motivate the audience to watch the play.)*

4. How would Shakespeare's audiences have reacted to the witches? *(People at that time believed in the existence of witches. They would have been intrigued and possibly fearful.)*

### Scene ii

1. What news has the captain brought to King Duncan? *(He relates how Macbeth and Banquo fought valiantly against the Norwegian king and how Macbeth killed the rebel, Macdonwald.)*

2. What further news is brought by Ross? *(He tells of the traitorous Thane of Cawdor's assistance to the King of Norway, and that the Norwegian king asked for a truce and agreed to pay ten thousand dollars to Scotland.)*

3. What is King Duncan's reaction to the news about Cawdor? *(He orders his death and says he will give his title to Macbeth.)*

### Scene iii

1. What do the witches discuss as they await Macbeth? *(One of the witches plans to harass a sailor because his wife wouldn't give her any chestnuts. The others offer to help her.)*

2. How do the witches surprise Macbeth and Banquo? *(They hail Macbeth with two titles he does not yet have—Thane of Cawdor and King "hereafter.")*

3. What do they tell Banquo? *(that he will be the father of kings)*

4. How could Banquo be "lesser than Macbeth, and greater," and "not so happy, yet much happier"? *(various answers)*

5. What does Macbeth demand of the witches? *(He wants to know the source of their prophecies, but they vanish.)*

6. What news does Ross relate? *(that Macbeth will receive the title of Thane of Cawdor)*

7. How do Macbeth and Banquo react differently to Ross's information? *(For Macbeth, it gives credence to the witches' prophecies. Banquo is more cautious and fears the witches will betray them in the end.)*

8. What does this line mean? "If chance will have me King, why chance may crown me without my stir." *(After briefly entertaining thoughts of murdering the king in order to gain the throne, Macbeth decides to leave it to chance.)*

### Scene iv

1. How did Cawdor die? *(in deep repentance)*

2. How had King Duncan always felt about Cawdor? *("He was a gentleman on whom I built an absolute trust.")* What does this tell you about Duncan's character? *(He is not a good judge of character, is too naive and trusting.)*

3. What announcement does King Duncan make after he, Macbeth, and Banquo exchange warm greetings? *(His son, Malcolm, is now Prince of Cumberland and heir to the throne.)*

14

4. How does Macbeth view the Prince of Cumberland? *(He is "a step on which I must fall down or else o'erleap," i.e., Malcolm is in his way and must be dealt with.)*

### Scene v
1. How was Lady Macbeth advised of the witches' prophecies? *(in a letter from Macbeth)*

2. What is Lady Macbeth's main concern about her husband? *(He is too kind and unambitious to take the easiest way to the throne, i.e. the murder of Duncan.)*

3. On whom does Lady Macbeth call for guidance and strength? *(evil spirits)*

4. What does Lady Macbeth mean by "He that's coming must be provided for"? *(She wants Macbeth to kill Duncan that night when he comes to their castle, Inverness.)*

### Scene vi
1. As Duncan arrives at Inverness, does he suspect that anything could be wrong? *(no)* How do you know? *("This castle hath a pleasant seat..." etc.)*

2. What is ironic about the way Duncan and Lady Macbeth speak? *(The king is totally trusting, and Lady Macbeth says all the expected social things, while in fact she is trying to convince her husband to kill him.)* Have you ever been in a situation where someone acted like Lady Macbeth? What was your reaction?

### Scene vii
1. What does Macbeth's long soliloquy at the beginning of this scene mean? *(He is listing all the reasons why he finds the proposed murder of Duncan such a horrific deed. He ends by saying he is motivated only by ambition.)*

2. What does Macbeth first tell Lady Macbeth? *("We will proceed no further in this business.")*

3. What methods does Lady Macbeth use to goad him into action? *(She asks him if he is a coward and accuses him of not being a man; she assures him she would kill her own baby if he wanted her to.)*

4. After reading the speech Lady Macbeth makes about her baby, what adjectives can you use to describe her? *(ruthless, ambitious, sinful, criminal, sick)*

5. What plan has Lady Macbeth formulated for Duncan's demise? *(She will drug his two chamberlains, leaving him unprotected. Macbeth will stab Duncan. The chamberlains will be blamed.)*

6. What does Macbeth add to the plan? *(He will use the guards' daggers to kill Duncan, and then smear the killers with blood.)*

## Topic for Writing

You have probably read your horoscope or perhaps experimented with some other form of trying to foretell the future. How much faith, if any, do you put in such things as astrology, palmistry, the Tarot, and ESP? Explain your answer.

## Prediction

Do you think the Macbeths' plan to kill Duncan will succeed? Will all the witches' prophecies come true, including the one about Banquo? How might this be possible?

## Act II

### Vocabulary

| Scene i | Scene ii | Scene iii | Scene iv |
|---|---|---|---|
| husbandry | fatal bellman | equivocator | entomb |
| summons | possets | anon | suborned |
| offices | confounds | stirring | ravin up |
| allegiance | infirm | obscure bird | invested |
| palpable | incarnadine | temple | storehouse |
| dudgeon | | countenance | benison |
| sentinel | | vault | |
| watch | | amiss | |
| horror | | breeched | |
| | | auger | |
| | | frailties | |
| | | malice | |

### Questions for Discussion

*Scene i*

1. At what time does this scene take place? What lines tell you? *(It is past midnight. "The moon is down; I have not heard the clock." "And she goes down at twelve.")*

2. Why would Banquo prefer not to sleep? *(He has been having dreams about the witches' predictions and doesn't like his own "cursed thoughts" on the matter.)*

3. What offer does Macbeth make to Banquo? *(He tells Banquo he'll reward him if he agrees to support Macbeth, but is unclear about what his intentions are. Banquo says he'll support his friend as long as he can keep his honor and his clear conscience. They plan to talk more later.)*

4. What feelings does Macbeth reveal in his soliloquy at the end of this scene? *(He is horrified at the vision of the bloody dagger, and hesitates in his resolve, then tells himself that words are a hindrance to the deed he must do.)*

## Scene ii

1. What feat has Lady Macbeth accomplished? *(She has drugged the grooms' bedtime drinks and they are in a stupor.)*

2. Lady Macbeth said she would have killed Duncan herself except for what? *(He reminded her of her father.)*

3. What does Macbeth tell his wife? *(He has killed Duncan.)*

4. What did Macbeth hear, or imagine he heard, while he was in Duncan's chamber? Can you explain this? *(He thought he heard someone cry "Murder!" "God bless us!" and "Amen!" as well as "Sleep no more! Macbeth does murder sleep.")*

5. In what ways does Lady Macbeth's reaction to the murder differ from Macbeth's? *(She is much more practical and it doesn't seem to bother her to go back for the daggers and bloody the grooms.)*

6. What advice does she give Macbeth? *("Consider it not so deeply.")*

7. Macbeth is overwhelmed with guilt over what he has done. What lines indicate this? *("Will all great Neptune's ocean wash this blood clean from my hand?" and "To know my deed, 'twere best not know myself./Wake Duncan with thy knocking! I would thou couldst," are especially revealing of Macbeth's remorse.)*

## Scene iii

1. Why do you think Shakespeare added the porter and his long speech? *(The porter adds comic relief while dramatic tension builds around the knocking on the door.)*

2. Besides being funny, is the porter's speech in any way ironic? *(He speaks of the gates of hell, the devil, treason, equivocation, and stealing. Macbeth has consorted with the agents of the devil, the witches, and is certainly guilty of treason, lying, and stealing the throne.)*

3. Who does the porter admit to the castle? *(Macduff and Lennox)*

4. As Lennox and Macbeth talk, what is Macduff about to do? *(discover Duncan)*

5. How does Macduff's treatment of Lady Macbeth strike you? *(Students should see the irony in Macduff's wish to protect the "gentlelady" from the hideous sight of the murdered king.)* How does she react? *(faints)*

6. What was Macbeth's reaction to the discovery? *(He feigned a terrible grief and quickly killed the grooms, blaming his rash actions on his love for the king.)*

7. What wise decision do Malcolm and Donalbain make? Why? *(They decide to leave, Malcolm to England and Donalbain to Ireland, thinking attempts on their lives may also be made.)*

*Scene iv*
1. Shakespeare often uses references to the weather and strange occurrences to create an ominous mood. Give examples of this from scene iv. *(The day is as dark as night; an owl killed a falcon, and Duncan's horses went wild and ate one another.)*

2. What might the Old Man in this scene represent? *(He is an agent from the village and represents the sentiments of the Scottish people.)*

3. Who is under suspicion for Duncan's murder? *(his sons)* Does this make any sense? *(various answers)*

4. Who will be king now? *(Macbeth)*

5. Explain the line, "Lest our old robes sit easier than our new!" *(Macduff has his doubts about Macbeth as a ruler.)*

**Topics for Writing**
1. Think about the line, "Macbeth does murder sleep." Why is sleep important? What effect would an inability to sleep have on someone who is already on edge? How does a lack of sleep affect you?

2. The scene where Macbeth actually kills Duncan is not included. Write that scene.

**Prediction**
Will Macbeth be discovered as the murderer? Is there anyone who might be suspicious of him? Will he confess?

## Act III

**Vocabulary**

| *Scene i* | *Scene ii* | *Scene iv* | *Scene v* |
|---|---|---|---|
| foully | scorched | measure | beldams |
| verities | eminence | nonpareil | saucy |
| oracles | vizards | casing | sprites |
| knit | jocund | mischance | |
| parricide | cloistered | authorized | *Scene vi* |
| rebuked | rooky | charnel houses | borne |
| unlineal | rouse | avaunt | broad words |
| utterance | | speculation | rue |
| gospelled | | | accursed |
| beggared | | | |
| clept | | | |
| valued file | | | |
| avouch | | | |
| clearness | | | |

## Questions for Discussion

### Scene i

1. Paraphrase Banquo's first speech in this scene. *(Macbeth, it happened just as the witches said, but I'm afraid it was you who murdered Duncan. Even so, they said that my sons, not yours, would be kings. If they spoke the truth for you, why not for me?)*

2. How does Macbeth find out Banquo's plans for the day? *(He invites him to a feast and finds out he'll be out until dark but will attend the banquet.)* Does Banquo suspect Macbeth of any ill will toward him? *(no)*

3. What has Macbeth realized about Banquo? *(Macbeth, who has no children, realizes he murdered Duncan so that Banquo's descendants can take the throne, if the witches were right.)*

4. Does Macbeth totally believe in the witches at this point? *(most will say yes)* Does he have good reason to? *(yes)*

5. How does Macbeth get the murderers on his side? *(He convinces them Banquo is their enemy.)*

6. What does Macbeth want the murderers to do? *(murder Banquo and his son, Fleance, when they return to the castle that evening for the feast)*

### Scene ii

1. How does Lady Macbeth try to comfort her husband? *(She tells him what's done is done and encourages him to be "bright and jovial" that evening.)*

2. Is Macbeth able to accept her advice? *(Not really—he says he will never be at peace, and is worried about Banquo. Lady Macbeth is unaware of the planned murders, making his consternation harder to understand.)*

3. From this scene, what is your evaluation of the Macbeth's relationship? *(Answers will vary, but most will see the tenderness between the two.)*

### Scene iii

1. Summarize this scene. *(The murderers descend on Banquo and Fleance. Banquo is killed, but Fleance gets away.)*

### Scene iv

1. How does Macbeth react to the news that Banquo's throat has been cut? *(He praises the murderer.)*

2. Why is Macbeth distressed by the escape of Fleance? *(This bothers him because of the prediction that Banquo's sons will rule, but he plans to kill Fleance later on.)*

3. What "surprise guest" appears at the feast? *(Banquo's ghost)*

4. What is Macbeth's reaction to the apparition? *(He is horrified and begins speaking what appears to be nonsense to his guests. Lady Macbeth makes excuses for him and finally asks the guests to leave.)*

5. Who is conspicuously NOT present at the feast? *(Macduff)*

6. What does "...in his house I keep a servant fee'd" mean? *(Macbeth pays a servant in Macduff's house to spy on him.)*

7. What does Macbeth plan to do as soon as possible? *(Find "the weird sisters" again and seek out their advice.)*

### Scene v
1. Who is Hecate and why is she angry? *(Queen of the Witches, Hecate is angry that the three weird sisters went ahead and made plans for Macbeth without her knowledge.)*

2. What is the effect of this scene? *(Macbeth's fate has now been turned over to the "head witch." Shakespeare's audiences would have been particularly aware of his deeper descent into evil at this point. We know the witches have plotted against him all along, just as Banquo warned after their first encounter.)*

### Scene vi
1. Lennox and other Thanes are now suspicious of Macbeth's role in the deaths of Duncan, the two guards, and Banquo. In this scene, what does Lennox reveal about Macduff? *(He has gone to England to meet with Malcolm and enlist the aid of the English king, Northumberland, and Siward in raising an army against Macbeth.)*

### Topic for Writing
Compare the personalities of Macbeth and his friend, Banquo, particularly in relation to their reaction to the witches and in the degree of ambition each exhibits.

### Activity
- Use the "Plot Structure of a Tragedy" map on page 25 of this guide to make a transparency for the overhead projector, or transfer the information to the board. Have the students use the blank map on page 26 to identify which scenes in *Macbeth* correspond to the divisions of the diagram. Have the students finish the diagram as the play unfolds.

  **Exposition**—Macbeth, Thane of Glamis, will be named Thane of Cawdor as well.
  **Exciting Force**—Macbeth and Banquo meet the witches.
  **Rising Action**—Macbeth kills Duncan and his guards, is crowned king, and has Banquo murdered.

**Turning Point**—Banquo's ghost appears; Macbeth begins to act very irrationally.

**Falling Action**—Macduff and Malcolm gather forces; Macbeth foolishly places his faith in the witches' predictions; the army advances on Macbeth's castle.

**Moment of Final Suspense**—Perhaps Macbeth will be saved ("No man of woman born...").

**Catastrophe**—Macduff kills Macbeth and brings his head to Malcolm.

## ACT IV

### Vocabulary

| Scene i | Scene ii | Scene iii |
|---|---|---|
| brinded | coz | birthdom |
| harpier | gin | redress |
| entrails | homely | dolor |
| venom | laudable | perchance |
| cauldron | folly | safeties |
| adder | unsanctified | affeered |
| slab | | impediments |
| yesty | | foisons |
| Nature's germains | | portable |
| harped | | at a point |
| vanquished | | stamp |
| bodements | | relation |
| sceptres | | nice |
| blood-boltered | | outlatch |
| pernicious | | |
| firstlings | | |

### Questions for Discussion

*Scene i*

1. What does Macbeth's anxiety to see the witches show? (*He has become dependent on them to foretell his future.*)

2. What are the first three apparitions to appear, and what does each tell Macbeth? (*The first, an armed head, tells Macbeth to beware Macduff. The second, a bloody child, assures him "none of woman born shall harm Macbeth." The third, a crowned child carrying a tree, tells Macbeth he will not be conquered until Birnam Wood moves to Dunsinane, an impossibility.*)

3. What is the final apparition? *(a procession of eight kings and Banquo, signifying the long line of Banquo's descendants who will control the kingdom)*

4. Why is it important that Macbeth learns of Macduff's plan for revenge right after he meets with the witches? *(This gives credence to the first prediction.)*

### Scene ii

1. Where does this scene take place? *(in Macduff's castle at Fife)*

2. What is Lady Macduff complaining about? *(that Macduff left her and his children and suddenly fled; She fears he doesn't love them.)*

3. On what do Lady Macduff and her son disagree? *(Lady Macduff believes her husband is a traitor and is probably dead; her son insists he is not a traitor and is alive.)*

4. What antithesis is found in this scene? *("...where to do harm/ Is often laudable, to do good sometimes/Accounted dangerous folly.")*

5. What is the outcome? *(Lady Macduff and her son are murdered. Since Macduff has more than one child, we must assume that they were all killed.)*

### Scene iii

1. Why does Malcolm tell Macduff that when he, Malcolm, becomes king, "black Macbeth/ Will seem as pure as snow" ? *(Malcolm is rather paranoid at this point, and wants to test Macduff's loyalty to his country before he puts his trust in him.)*

2. How does Macduff convince Malcolm he can be trusted? *(He reminds him of his sainted father and mother, bemoans the fate of his beloved Scotland.)*

3. What information does Ross have for Macduff? *(that his wife and children have been murdered)* What is Macduff's reaction? *(He is distraught with grief and more determined than ever to wreak revenge on Macbeth.)*

4. What help has the English king offered Malcolm and Macduff?
*(ten thousand soldiers)*

**Topic for Writing**
Reread Lady Macduff's speech beginning, "I am in this earthly world...folly."
Paraphrase this speech, and then give examples from your own experience as proof that the thoughts expressed can often be true.

**Prediction**
Will Macduff and Malcolm succeed, or will Macbeth reign victorious? What do you want to happen in the last act?

# ACT V

## Vocabulary

| *Scene i* | *Scene iii* | *Scene v* | *Scene viii* |
|---|---|---|---|
| gentlewoman | epicures | famine | Roman fool |
| guise | patch | ague | intrenchant |
| charged | moe | fell of hair | vulnerable crests |
| annoyance | skirr | dismal treatise | baited |
| mated | physic | | knell |
| | cast | *Scene vi* | knolled |
| *Scene ii* | pristine | screens | kingdom's pearl |
| alarm | purgative | harbingers | kinsmen |
| faith-breach | | | |
| sickly weal | *Scene iv* | *Scene vii* | |
| sovereign flower | censures | tied me to a stake | |
| | soldiership | kerns | |
| | | bruited | |
| | | gently rend'red | |

## Questions for Discussion

### Scene i

1. Why has the doctor been called to Dunsinane? *(to attend Lady Macbeth, who is walking in her sleep)*

2. What motion does Lady Macbeth make continuously? *(She rubs her hands together, as if washing them.)*

3. In your own words, what is the doctor's evaluation of Lady Macbeth's problem? *(She is suffering from a malady that only God can help her with, by forgiving her crimes.)*

### Scene ii

1. Who are Menteith, Caithness, and Angus? *(Scottish noblemen who have joined the others in the fight against Macbeth)*

2. Why is it significant that Macbeth is now referred to as a <u>tyrant</u>? *(We realize how much he is detested by his countrymen.)* Does he have the support of those he commands? *(Not really—they have no heart for fighting, but are afraid not to.)*

3. What does the clothing imagery mean ("Now does he feel his title/ Hang loose about him...")? *(Macbeth is not worthy of the title he has assumed.)*

### Scene iii

1. What reports does the servant bring Macbeth, or try to? *(He tells him there are ten thousand English soldiers advancing toward Dunsinane.)*

2. Why does Macbeth make light of the servant's reports? *(He has put his faith in the prophecies of the apparitions, and feels invincible.)*

3. Will Macbeth be happy as long as he holds on to this title? *(no)* How do you know? *(He realizes he has no honor, love, obedience, or friends, but only the curses of those he rules.)*

4. Macbeth wishes the doctor could somehow remove from Lady Macbeth's (and perhaps his own) memory the knowledge of their deeds. Have you ever felt like that?

5. What does the doctor wish? *(that he was not at Dunsinane)*

*Scene iv*
1. Why does Malcolm tell the soldiers to cut boughs from the trees in Birnam Wood? *(to use as camouflage so Macbeth will not detect the advancement of so many soldiers)*

*Scene v*
1. What happens at the beginning of this scene? *(Macbeth is told that Lady Macbeth has died.)*

2. How does Macbeth react? *(He seems rather indifferent, perhaps realizing she is better off dead than suffering in her madness.)*

3. Paraphrase Macbeth's soliloquy following the announcement of his wife's death. *(He realizes how insignificant the brief life of one person is when compared to the eons of time, and he seems to be saying that all men are fools and their lives meaningless.)*

4. What message is delivered to Macbeth? *(that Birnam Wood is moving toward the castle)* What effect does this have on Macbeth? *(He begins to worry but resolves to fight.)*

*Scenes vi, vii*
1. What are the attitudes of Siward and Macduff as they prepare to fight? *(They are determined to give it all they have; Macduff is especially confident they will be victors.)*

2. Why is Macbeth unafraid of Young Siward? *(because of the prophecy regarding "woman born of man")*

3. What spurs Macduff on with such determination? *(the memory of his slain family)*

*Scene viii*
1. Explain the line, "Of all men else I have avoided thee!" *(Macbeth would really prefer not to have to kill Macduff, since he is already stained with the guilt of exterminating Macduff's whole family.)*

2. What surprise does Macbeth learn from Macduff? *(Macduff is the product of a Caesarean birth and thus is not "born of woman.")*

3. Does Macbeth give up when he realizes he has been tricked by the witches? *(no)*

4. What "prize" does Macduff bring to Malcolm? *(Macbeth's head)*

5. Who will now be King of Scotland? *(Malcolm)*

# Plot Structure of a Tragedy

**Climax or Turning Point:** the highest point of action in the play. Change in the protagonist, who seems now to be following a downward path.

**Rising Action:** series of events leading up to the climax; usually covers more than one act.

**Falling Action:** series of events following the climax; the conflict is the essense of the play; most events go against the protagonist.

**Exciting (or Inciting) Force:** Something happens that gets the action moving, usually in the first act.

**Moment of Final Suspense:** Near the end of the play, it begins to look as if things will go the way of the protagonist after all.

**Exposition:** the introductory section of a play in which time, place, characters, and situation are presented.

**Catastrophe:** the complete downfall of the protagonist, either through death or some other devastating experience.

# MACBETH
## PLOT MAP

**EXPOSITION:**


**EXCITING (OR INCITING) FORCE:**


**RISING ACTION:**




**CLIMAX OR TURNING POINT:**


**FALLING ACTION:**




**MOMENT OF FINAL SUSPENSE:**


**CATASTROPHE:**

# Post-Reading Questions
## for Discussion and Writing

1. Consider each of the following feelings/themes and decide how it is represented in *Macbeth*. Give one or more examples of each.

| | | | |
|---|---|---|---|
| evil | deception | disloyalty | pride |
| temptation | insanity | desire | confusion |
| determination | illusion | envy | anger |
| revenge | despair | passion | humility |
| love | injustice | courage | compassion |
| conceit | hatred | panic | fear |

2. *Macbeth* is often considered a morality play. What moral lessons would Shakespeare's audiences have taken with them after viewing the play? *(The play would probably have confirmed the following moral standards for Elizabethans: Be loyal to one's king and country; don't be ambitious for things you're not meant to have; don't consort with witches or other evil agents; if you are guilty of a crime, you will be punished one way or another.)*

3. Do you identify with Macbeth at the beginning of the play? at the end? How and why did your feelings change as the play unfolded?

4. Why is *Macbeth* considered a tragedy? Does Macbeth fit the definition of a tragic hero?

5. How does Lady Macbeth change over the course of the play? Do you feel sorry for her, or do you think she got what she deserved? Have you ever gotten away with doing something wrong and then been plagued by guilt over it? How did it feel compared to getting caught?

6. Use T-diagrams on the chalkboard to compare and contrast the following pairs of characters: Banquo/Macbeth, Macbeth/Lady Macbeth, Malcolm/Macduff, Duncan/Macbeth. Choose one pair and use the diagram as the basis for an essay.

7. Find references to darkness and light in the play. What do they symbolize? *(evil/good)*

8. How is a tyrant different from a benevolent ruler? Think about some tyrants in recent history. What happened to them in the end? Do you see a pattern?

# Creative Writing Suggestions

1. Rewrite *Macbeth* in the form of a fairy tale that would be understood by third-grade children. You might make the tale into a book with illustrations. If possible, present the story to a group of children and report their reactions.

2. It is implied that Lady Macbeth took her own life. Write the suicide note she left behind.

3. Write a scene referred to in the play which occurs offstage, i.e., the meeting between Malcolm and King Edward, the actual murder of Duncan, or one of Lady Macbeth's earlier sleepwalking episodes. As an alternate activity, write a scene that does not occur but might have. Suggestions: the Macbeth servants whisper about what they heard and saw the night Duncan died; Fleance runs home and reports his father's murder.

4. Write a five-stanza poem summarizing the main events of each act of the play, one stanza per act.

5. Choose a popular song and change the lyrics to celebrate the victory of Macduff over Macbeth and the crowning of Malcolm.

6. You are the doctor called to Macbeth's castle to tend Lady Macbeth. Write your observations of her symptoms, your diagnosis, a suggested treatment, and a prognosis.

7. Make up some political jokes that might have circulated in Scotland while Macbeth was king. (Examples: Lady Macbeth to her lady-in-waiting: "Is it hot in here or am I just crazy?"; Macbeth to the doctor: "I swear I'll pay every cent I owe you, or Birnam Wood will come to Dunsinane.")

8. Tape a between-classes conversation you have with a friend or two. Rewrite the conversation in Shakespearean language. Enlist the help of your friends to tape your rewrite. Play both versions for the class.

9. Create one or two articles for the *Cawdor Enquirer.* Some suggested headlines:
   - *Exclusive Interview With Malcolm in England*
   - *Macduff Mourns Losses*
   - *Doctor Rules Lady Macbeth's Death a Suicide*
   - *Murderers Confess: Hired to Kill Banquo*
   - *Servant Recalls the Night of Duncan's Murder*
   - *She Confessed All While Sleepwalking*

10. Write an advertisement for one or more of the following:
    - Lady Macbeth Stain Remover
    - Genuine Assassin's Daggers
    - Clothing, Some Holes and Stains, Several Sizes
    - Royal Robes, Large Size
    - Prophecies by the Weird Sisters: Accuracy Guaranteed
    - Castle for Sale: Charming Glamis Location
    - The Sorcerer's Source: Supplies for All Spells

11. Write epitaphs for all the characters who died in *Macbeth.*

12. Imagine you are in charge of filling a time capsule to be buried in the Scottish capital, Scone, on the day Malcolm is crowned. Make a list of what you will put in the time capsule.

13. Make a list of Shakespearean insults, for instance Macduff's son calls the murderer a "shag-eared villain" and Macbeth calls his servant a "lily-livered boy." Once you have a list of adjective-noun insults, switch the adjectives around to make some new insults.

14. Choose one of the long soliloquies in *Macbeth,* and translate it into a rap song with approximately the same meaning.

15. Change the setting of *Macbeth* to Washington, D.C. Choose an appropriate scene and rewrite it using modern characters, situation, and language. (Example: Macbeth becomes Max Beckwith, corrupt senator, whose shady activities have just become known to his constituents. Max finds a reader of Tarot cards at a flea market, and immediately employs her full-time, using government funds, to foretell his future.)

29

# Extension Activities

## Suggested Passages for Memorization and Oral Presentation:
In the interest of fairness, you might offer a higher grade for the longest passages.

| | | |
|---|---|---|
| I, iii | Macbeth | "This supernatural soliciting…<br>…and nothing is but what is not." |
| I, v | Lady Macbeth | "Glamis thou art…<br>…to have thee crowned withal." |
| I, vii | Lady Macbeth | "What beast was't then…<br>Have done to this." |
| II, i | Macbeth | "Is this a dagger which I see…<br>…too cold breath gives." |
| II, iii | Porter | "Here's a knocking indeed!…<br>…remember the porter." |
| III, i | Banquo | "Thou hast it now—…<br>…But hush, no more!" |
| III, iv | Macbeth | "It will have blood, they say:…<br>…What is the night?" |
| IV, i | Witches, Hecate | "Thrice the brinded cat…<br>…all that you put in." |
| IV, ii | Lady Macduff | "Whither should I fly?…<br>…What are these faces?" |
| IV, iii | Macduff | "Fit to govern?…<br>…Thy hope ends here!" |
| IV, iii | Ross | "Alas, poor country,<br>…Dying or ere they sicken." |
| V, i | Lady Macbeth | "Out damned spot!<br>…had so much blood in him?" |
| V, iii | Macbeth | "Seyton!—I am sick at heart,<br>…and dare not. Seyton!" |
| V, v | Macbeth | "She should have died hereafter…<br>…signifying nothing." |
| V, viii | Macduff | "Hail, King, for so thou art…<br>…Hail, King of Scotland!" |

# For Further Reading and Viewing

Film Versions:  *Macbeth* (1948)  Starring and directed by Orson Welles
                *Macbeth* (1971)  Starring Jon Finch, directed by Roman Polanski

## Activities

1. View one of the film versions of the play and evaluate it from two standpoints: How well does it portray the characters and plot? and, How good is it as a stand-alone movie?

2. View or read another Shakespeare tragedy *(Hamlet, Othello, Julius Caesar)* and compare the characters and themes with those in *Macbeth.* You might also compare your reactions to the main characters, i.e., whether or not you identify with them and want them to avoid their tragic ends.

# Additional Subject Areas

## Art
- Sketch a portrait of one of the main characters.
- Design a book jacket for a collection of Shakespeare's tragedies.
- Clip magazine pictures of models you think would be good in the roles of Lady Macbeth, Macbeth, Banquo, Macduff, Malcolm, Ross, and other characters.
- Use magazine clippings to make a collage representing one of the play's themes or the setting.
- Create a comic strip depicting an important scene from the play, including dialogue balloons.
- Design a t-shirt you might purchase at a Macbeth play that was touring Scotland.

## Computer Graphics/Desktop Publishing
- Using articles, advertisements, and artwork created by classmates, prepare a layout for a newspaper published a few days after Macbeth's defeat. Produce the paper and distribute it to your class and other English classes.

## Research
- Find out about Scotland today. What type of terrain exists there? What products are manufactured? What agricultural is most common? What are Scotland's natural resources? What problems affect Scotland today?

## Culinary Arts
- Create a menu for the feast held to celebrate Macbeth's takeover of the throne.
- Create a recipe folder of Scotch foods.

## Science
- The doctor called to aid Lady Macbeth said there was nothing he could do for her. Compare common medical practices in Shakespeare's day with those of today. What would today's doctors do for Lady Macbeth?

## History
- Witches were actively sought out and executed in Shakespeare's day. Later on, the famous Salem witch trials took place in America. Find out more about witchcraft in England and America in the 16th and 17th centuries.

## Language
- A compulsive hand-washer is often said to have a "Lady Macbeth" complex. Make a poster listing other terms and phrases from Shakespeare plays which are in common use today.

## Drama/Music
- With a partner or group, make a rock video depicting the main events of Macbeth. Choose music that is adaptable to the theme.

## Current Events
- Find examples of incidents involving the following in this month's magazines and newspapers: revenge, insanity, deception, injustice, tyranny, ambition, courage, disloyalty. Make a poster of your clippings.

# Using Character Attribute Webs

Attribute webs are simply a visual representation of a character's traits. They provide a systematic way for students to organize and recap the information they have about that particular character. Attribute webs may be used after reading the story or completed gradually as information unfolds—done individually, or finished as a group project.

One type of character web uses these categories:

- **How a character acts and feels** (What do his/her statements reveal about feelings? What does his/her behavior show you about him/her? In a play: what do the character's gestures, facial expressions, tone of voice tell you about his/her emotions?)

- **How a character looks** (What do clothing and physique tell you about this character?)

- **Where a character lives** (In what country, state, neighborhood, does this character live? During what time period?)

- **How others feel about the character** (What do others' statements and actions show about their attitude toward the character?)

In group discussion about the student attribute webs for specific characters, the teacher can ask for supportive evidence from the story.

Attribute webs need not be confined to characters. They can also be used to organize information about a concept, object, or place.

Attribute webs are a kind of semantic mapping. Students can move on from attribute webs to other creative kinds of mapping. They can be encouraged to modify attribute webs—use sub-divisions, add divisions, change connections—in whatever ways are useful to them personally. It is important to emphasize that attribute webs are just a graphic way to record ideas. They provide students with a tool for helping them generate ideas and think about relationships among them.

> **Activity:** Have the students begin attribute webs for Macbeth and/or Lady Macbeth. You might also have them meet in groups to create webs organized around a central idea in the play, such as ambition, jealousy, revenge, fear, etc. See the suggested frameworks which follow.

# Sample frameworks

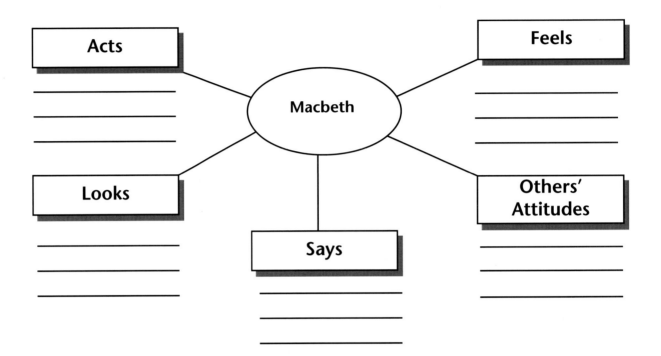

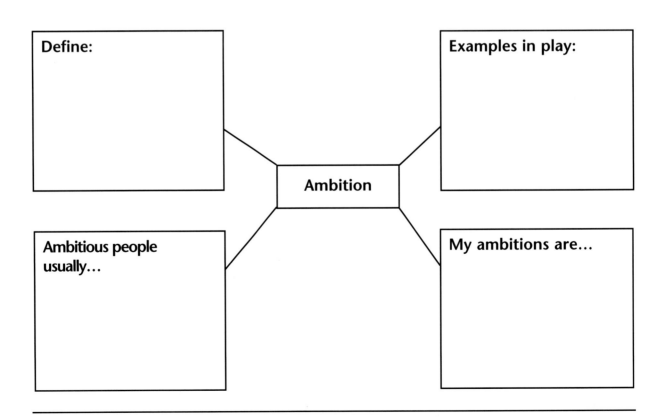

34

# Evaluation: Rubric for Essay-Writing

The following is a suggested set of criteria for student essays. Students find it helpful for self-evaluation before turning in an assignment, and you may find it helpful for determining grades. We encourage you to share the evaluation sheets with students <u>before</u> they write their essays.

| Criterion | Maximum # of points total: 100 |
|---|---|
| 1. *Focus:* Student writes a clear thesis and includes it in the opening paragraph. | 10 |
| 2. *Organization:* The final draft reflects the assigned outline; transition words are used to link ideas. | 15 |
| 3. *Support:* Sufficient details are cited to support the thesis; extraneous details are omitted. | 15 |
| 4. *Detail:* Each quote or reference is explained (as if the teacher had not read the book); ideas are not redundant. | 15 |
| 5. *Mechanics:* Spelling, capitalization, usage are correct. | 15 |
| 6. *Sentence structure:* The student avoids run-ons and fragments. There is an interesting variety of sentences. | 10 |
| 7. *Verbs:* All verbs are in the correct tense; sections in which plot is summarized are in the present tense. | 10 |
| 8. *Total effect of the essay:* clarity, coherence, overall effectiveness. | 10 |

**Total Score:** _____

**Comments:**

# Assessment for *Macbeth*

Assessment is an ongoing process. The following ten items can be completed during the *Macbeth* study. Once finished, the student and teacher will check the activities. Points may be added to indicate the level of understanding.

Name _____ Date _____

**Student**     **Teacher**

_____     _____     1.  Make a listing of the characters from the play, noting when they were introduced, relationship to other characters, and key description useful to a casting agent.

_____     _____     2.  Create a plot summary and plot graph for the play including exposition, exciting force, rising action, climax, falling action, moment of final suspense, and catastrophe.

_____     _____     3.  List new vocabulary words you have learned while reading the play.

_____     _____     4.  Create attribute webs for Macbeth and Lady Macbeth.

_____     _____     5.  Record ideas on ambition, power, guilt, and ruthlessness. Use a web. Be sure to include ideas and examples from the play as well as elsewhere.

_____     _____     6.  Keep your writing done in response to reading the play in a folder. Choose two pieces to revise and submit for evaluation. See evaluation rubric on page 35.

_____     _____     7.  Choose one of the creative writing suggestions on pages 28 and 29 for a bit of fun.

_____     _____     8.  Memorize a bit of *Macbeth.* See suggestions on page 30.

_____     _____     9.  Choose one of the interdisciplinary activities on pages 31 and 32.

_____     _____     10. Why is *Macbeth* so often taught in high schools? Answer in a letter to a college-age friend.